BOOK 3

HEADWORK

Chris Culshaw and Deborah Waters

OXFORD UNIVERSITY PRESS

Oxford University Press, Walton Street, Oxford OX2 6DP

Oxford New York Toronto
Delhi Bombay Calcutta Madras Karachi
Petaling Jaya Singapore Hong Kong Tokyo
Nairobi Dar es Salaam Cape Town
Melbourne Auckland

and associated companies in
Berlin Ibadan Nicosia

Oxford is a trade mark of Oxford University Press

© Oxford University Press 1984

First published 1984

Reprinted 1984, 1985, 1987, 1988, 1990

ISBN 0 19 833374 9

Illustrations are by Andy Bylo,
Marie-Hélène Jeeves, Hugh Marshall,
David Murray, and Ursula Sieger

The cover illustration is by
Marie-Hélène Jeeves

Typeset in Great Britain by
Rowland Phototypesetting Ltd
Bury St Edmunds, Suffolk
and printed by
Scotprint, Musselburgh

CONTENTS

Headwork is based on the following assumptions:

> that we learn to read by reading;
>
> that reading is in essence a problem solving process;
>
> that different types of reading matter demand different strategies.

The books have been written to help pupils find a challenge in the necessary routine of practising basic reading skills and to help them understand that reading involves thinking. We have therefore tried to balance readability against "thinkability" and posed demanding questions in an interesting but readable way.

Most of the tasks have a puzzle element and often ask the pupil to read with a specific question in mind. Some ask the learner to restructure what s/he has read by changing text into drawing. Some demand comparison between pictures or between texts. Some require summaries. Others involve sequencing. Many are designed to develop skills of classification and introduce different ways of tabulating information.

While many of the tasks lead to clear-cut, short (often single word) written answers, others are more open-ended and ask the pupil to use concepts such as "true", "false" and "not enough evidence" and later: "probably true", "probably false" and "definitely true" or "definitely false". These open-ended tasks lend themselves to oral work in pairs or in small groups.

There is constant repetition of basic sight words and concepts including colours, shapes, parts of the body, and terms that define position in time and space such as *over*, *under*, *next to*, *before*, *after*, *right*, *left*, etc.

In compiling *Headwork* we have been concerned above all to help learners in their efforts to *comprehend* what they read. So, text is supported with pictures and diagrams and new and difficult words are introduced in meaningful contexts.

"Readability" measures have many shortcomings and do not always do justice to the subtlety of the reading process. It is difficult to say exactly what makes a text readable and comprehensible: factors such as syntax, topic, concept loading, the match between the text and the readers' prior knowledge all play a part. Simple texts, with strictly controlled vocabulary, are not always the easiest to read with understanding. What is more, such texts offer very little challenge and may well defeat our ends for they are unlikely to get our pupils reading and *re-reading* in their efforts to search for meaning. There must be some challenge, some puzzlement and intellectual demand if the pupil is to develop into a reflective reader.

The table shows the major skills practised by each task. This is a broad categorization as the categories often overlap. For example, many of the matching tasks also require sequencing skills. The table also identifies those tasks which need a lot of teacher input, both in starting the learners off and in discussing their answers.

Major skills emphasized	page number
Cloze	10, ⑫, ㉑, 24, 32, 33, 42
Drawing from text	25, **35**, 64
Matching	6, 8, 9, 14–15, 28–29, ㉚–㉛, 38, 64
Deduction	11, 16–17, **23**, 40–41, 43, 44–45, **㊿–(51)**
Sequencing	26, 34, 36–37, 54
Classification	**30–31**, (62), 63
Flow charts	27, 39, 53
Homonyms	47, 55
Summary	**48–49**, 56, 58–59
Solving riddles	7, **13**, 18, 19, 20, 22, **46**, **(57)**
Comparisons	52, 60–61

Numbers printed in **bold** indicate tasks needing a lot of teacher explanation.
Numbers circled indicate tasks with open-ended outcomes and a number of possible answers.

What to do

Name the giant reptiles. Use the descriptions underneath.

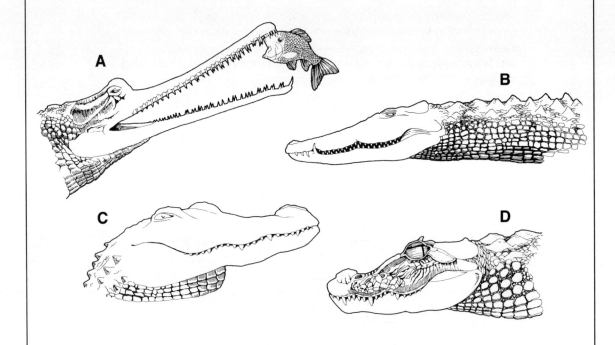

1. The **alligator** has a long, fat nose.   All its bottom teeth are hidden by its top teeth when its mouth is shut.

2. The **gavial** has a long nose like a saucepan handle.   It eats fish.   It catches them on its long teeth.   It has more teeth than any of the other giant reptiles.

3. The **crocodile** has a thin nose.   When its jaws are shut nearly all its teeth can be seen.   The fourth tooth back in the bottom jaw is longer than the others.   It can be seen sticking up even when the jaws are shut.

4. The **caiman** has a short fat nose.   Its teeth are long and pointed.   The top teeth hide the bottom teeth when its mouth is shut.

WOULD YOU LIKE ANYTHING ELSE, SIR?

What to do

Can you tell what **jobs** these people do from the things they say?

1. Do you want chips or rice?

2. I've got a parcel for Mrs Smith – does she live here?

3. Hold it still while I cut the leg off.

4. I'd better go and put my make-up on.   The show starts in ten minutes.

5. Can you see between its teeth?

6. Don't walk on that, please. It's still wet.

7. What's that word?

8. Are you eighteen?

9. No standing up please.

10. Is this your dog, madam?

11. When did you first notice the rash?

12. Open wide please.

13. Don't smile until he says, "I love you."

14. Have you anything to declare?

15. Don't use too much of that stuff or the whole place will go up!

RIDDLES

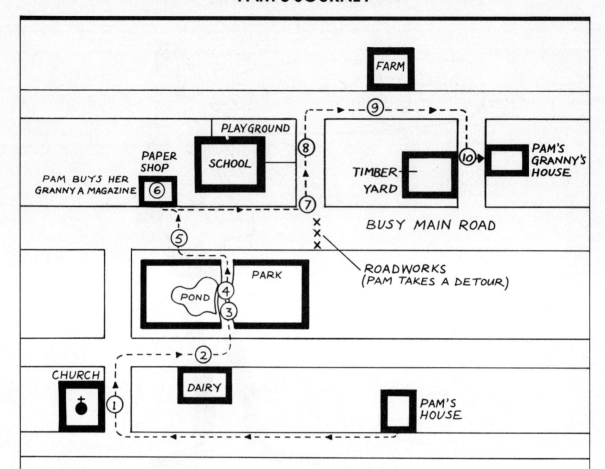

What to do

Pam is blind. This map shows a journey she made from her house to her granny's house. Here are ten sounds she heard as she walked along. Can you put them in the right order? Match the sounds with the numbers on the map.

Sounds:

A. An electric saw

B. A road mender's drill

C. Ducks

D. Children playing netball

E. Hedge clippers and lawn mowers

F. A shop till

G. The bleep of a Pelican crossing

H. A church organ

I. Milk bottles rattling

J. A tractor

MATCHING

What to do

Who put these adverts in the paper?   Match the names below with the number next to the advert.

1. Strong oak coffin for sale.   One owner.   Very old.   In excellent condition except for one or two blood stains.

2. Two black capes for sale – one large and one small.   Also two black masks.   Ideal for fancy dress.

3. Warm, woolly suit.   Bright green.   It will fit a small child (or a large frog).   Not water-proof.

4. Red and white suit for sale.   Also one reindeer – one careful owner.

5. Lots of old-fashioned clothes for sale.   Most are in good condition, but some have gunpowder on them.

6. Tight fitting blue suits with red capes.   Large sizes only.

7. For sale as a job lot: 10 green suits with matching hats.   Ideal for fancy dress.   Also bows and arrows going cheap.

8. One blue police box; rather old but it will take you anywhere.   Why pay £'s on bus fares?

9. For sale – one large rabbit hole, with all mod. cons.   Quick sale needed – owner has to go to Hollywood.

10. For sale: one red and black striped pullover.   It has some rips but it could be mended.

The advertisers:

A. Dr Who
B. Father Christmas
C. Bugs Bunny
D. Dennis the Menace
E. Guy Fawkes

F. Superman
G. Kermit the Frog
H. Count Dracula
I.   Robin Hood
J. Batman

MATCHING

What to do

Find the missing words.

One night, two men were walking through a ___1___ . It was dark. One of the men said:

"I do not like this place."

But his ___2___ said:

"We are mates and if we stick together we will be ___3___ ."

Then a big ___4___ came along. The first man jumped up a tree. He did not ___5___ about his mate. The second man was left on his ___6___ . He lay down on the ground, very still. He knew a ___7___ will not eat a dead body.

The bear walked up to the man on the ground. He ___8___ his body. He sniffed at his nose, his ___9___ and his ears. The bear thought the man was dead, ___10___ he went away.

The first man came ___11___ from the tree. He said:

"I saw the bear put his mouth to your ___12___ . What did he say?"

The second man said:

"He told the truth – not like ___13___ !"

" ___14___ do you mean?" said his mate.

"He told me not to trust a ___15___ who runs off at the first sign of danger."

Moral:
A friend in need is a friend indeed.

What to do

Answer true (T), false (F) or not enough evidence (NEE).
Write your answers like this: 1. *False*

1. There are three cups on the table.

2. The bread is stale.

3. There are two plants on the oven.

4. The washing powder is on the floor.

5. There are two bottles in the cupboard.

6. The brush is by the wall.

7. The knife is between the vase and the loaf.

8. The bucket is under the table.

9. There are two plants on the top of the fridge.

10. The plates are near the clock.

11. The kitchen door has a broken lock.

12. There is a small bottle of pills on the top shelf in the cupboard.

13. The plants are next to the candle.

14. The cup is on the left of the teapot.

15. There is a cat in the sink.

16. The cooker has an eye level grill.

17. There is a bottle of coke in the cupboard.

18. There are two glasses in the cupboard.

DEDUCTION

What to do

Find the missing words or phrases.
Write your answers like this: *1. Where are you going?*

Bill	Hello.
Tom	Hello.
Bill	1 ?
Tom	To the pictures.
Bill	2 ?
Tom	Star Wars, I think.
Bill	What time does it start?
Tom	3 .
Bill	It will tell you in the paper.
Tom	Will you come with me?
Bill	Yes, if I can get some money.
Tom	4 ?
Bill	No, she gave me some yesterday.
Tom	Will your dad give you some?
Bill	No fear!
Tom	5 ?
Bill	I broke a window in his greenhouse.
Tom	6 ?
Bill	I was throwing the ball for our dog.
Tom	Oh dear. You won't be able to come with me.
Bill	7 ?
Tom	Sorry, I've only got enough for myself.
Bill	8 .
Tom	See you later.

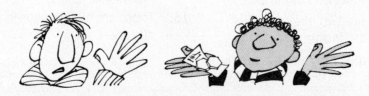

What to do

Harry Wasp is a very silly person. Instead of saying: "Can I have some fish and chips?" he would say: "Can I have some **f** and **c**?" He uses the first letter of a word to stand for a word. Here are some things Harry said. What do they mean?

Write your answers like this: *1. salt and vinegar*

1. I'd like some **s** and **v** on my chips.
2. I always have **b** and **e** for breakfast.
3. All the **b** and **g** had to line up for the fire practice.
4. **S** and **i** covered the pitch so we couldn't do games.
5. The people at the wedding got very drunk and began to **d** and **s**.
6. The little boy was frightened by the **t** and **l** so he ran inside.
7. The man ran through **s** and **f** to rescue his baby from the burning house.
8. The house was very old and did not have a **b** or **t**.
9. The cook put too much **s** and **p** in the stew.
10. The bomb wrecked the house. It blew the **d** and **w** off.
11. The man was dying. He asked for **p** and **p** so that he could write his will.

Oh dear, it's raining c and d

H.W.

RIDDLES

What to do

Match the signs with the speech balloons.
Write your answers like this: A. 4

A. I'll ask the man if we can go for a sail on the lake.

B. It's coming down now.

C. There is not anyone here to serve us. Ring that bell.

D. This is a very noisy camp site. I didn't sleep last night.

E. We must get some petrol somewhere.

F. Have you any change? I may have to pay.

G. That door should NOT be locked in case there is a fire.

H. Escalators make me dizzy.

I. Gosh! Look at all that soap coming out of the machine.

J. Put that out please! This is a hospital.

K. Do you think the doctor is in his office?

L. This shop closes at lunch time. What a nuisance! We'll have to wait.

MATCHING

①
Ring for Service

②
NO SMOKING

③
UP PRESS DOWN

④
BOATS FOR HIRE

⑤
STAND ON THE RIGHT

⑥
DO NOT OVERLOAD MACHINE

⑦
closed

⑧
Please KNOCK

⑨
TOILETS

⑩
at lunch BACK SOON

⑪
EMERGENCY EXIT

⑫
Camping

MATCHING

Answer true (T), false (F) or not enough evidence (NEE).

1. There are two bikes under the bridge.
2. There is a woman coming down the steps.
3. The motor boat is called 'The Black Swan'.
4. There is a woman mending a boat by the canal.
5. The man sitting by the motor boat has caught a fish.
6. The man sitting in the motor boat has been fishing.
7. The woman mending the boat is wearing glasses.
8. There are four broken canoes in the club shed.
9. The water in the canal is over 3 metres deep.
10. The bridge over the canal is more than a hundred years old.

11. The girl in the canoe under the bridge is wearing a lifejacket.
12. One of the windows in the canoe club is broken.
13. Both people on the steps are holding bags.
14. All the canoes have numbers.
15. Both cats are sitting on the canal bank.
16. One of the men standing on the canal bridge is wearing a hat.
17. Both dogs are on the same side of the canal.
18. One of the bikes near the canoe club has no front wheel.
19. Both girls sitting on the edge of the canal are wearing shoes.
20. All the people on the canal bridge are watching the canoeists.

DEDUCTION

> **What to do**
>
> Can you tell what jobs these people do from the things they say?

1. What's in the net?   Is it a shark?
2. Get back into bed at once, Mr Smith!
3. Is this your motor bike, son?
4. Smile please.
5. I'm coming up.   I'm running out of air.
6. Have you got the ring?
7. Read the chart from the top please.
8. No, you never get hold of the mane.   You must hold the saddle.   Watch me.
9. And now ladies and gentlemen, we present the Dalton Brothers, those daring death defying dare-devils on the high wire . . .
10. Black or white coffee, sir?
11. It's a girl, Mrs Smith.   Just what you wanted.
12. That's it!   Keep your head up, but kick your legs.
13. I'd like to ask you some questions about your wife's disappearance.
14. Do you want 3-star or 4-star, madam?
15. Stand well back.   I'm nearly through and it's going to fall your way.
16. These should have been back last week.   I'm afraid there is 20p to pay.
17. Do you have any pain here when you eat?
18. We cannot land here.   There are too many rocks.
19. This sword was used to cut off the head of King Charles I.
20. How long will you be staying, sir?

What to do

Can you identify these 10 things?

1. I start off long, but end up short.
   I am all over the school.
   Teachers use me.

2. I am small.
   I am made of paper.
   I like to be in a safe place.
   I have a face hidden inside me.

3. I am small and round.
   I am usually hard.
   I am tied up with a chain, but I could never run away.
   I live in your kitchen or your bathroom.

4. You can see me, but you cannot touch me.
   You only see me when there is rain and sunshine at the same time.
   I am very colourful.

5. People live in us, sometimes.
   We are tall.
   We help ships.
   We are always by the sea.

6. You can open me with a knife.
   You close me with water.
   I can be any colour, but I am usually white.
   I carry messages.

7. Parts of me can be very hot.
   If you put things in me or on me they change.
   Be careful how you use me.
   I can be found in most homes.

8. I am long like a snake.
   I am flexible.
   I have a row of small holes near one end.
   I have a sharp metal spike near the other.
   People wear me.

9. I am metal.
   I am strong.
   I have a pair of locks.
   When I go round your wrist you're in trouble.

10. You see me on TV lit by a strong light.
    I am green and brown.
    I have pockets, but no hands to put in them.
    I am a table, but no one would eat off me.

RIDDLES

What to do

If objects could speak, what would they say?
Can you guess which objects might say these things?

1. Don't wind me up so hard.   It gives me a headache!
2. I hate winter.   I get mud and snow on me.
3. Help, I'm running out of gas!
4. No wonder I'm red hot.   You left me on all night.
5. It's time you cleaned me.   I could cause an accident.
6. You have left me behind again.   You will have to climb in through the window.
7. No wonder you hit the tree.   You haven't checked me for weeks.
8. Give me a drink!   I'm running out of steam.
9. Without me, you would have to work all your sums out in your head.
10. Every time you break me, you shorten my life.   Be careful!
11. Ouch . . .!!!   Use my handle.   Don't kick me open with your foot!
12. I remember every word you say to me.   No human memory can do that.

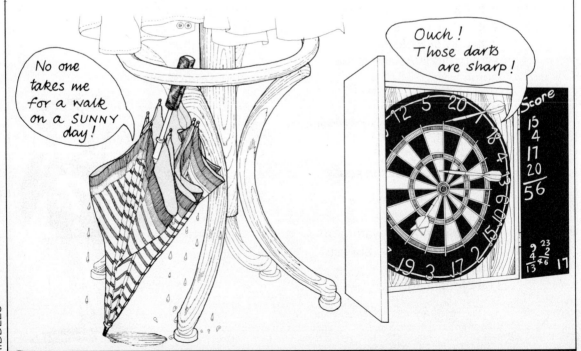

What to do

Find the missing words or phrases.
Write your answers like this: 1. *Hello*

Pam	Hello.
Mary	1 .
Pam	2 ?
Mary	To the fair. Do you want to come?
Pam	No. It's boring.
Mary	Haven't you heard about the new ride?
Pam	What new ride?
Mary	3 .
Pam	What's that?
Mary	It's like a roller coaster but you go upside down.
Pam	4 ?
Mary	You are strapped in.
Pam	5 ?
Mary	Yes. I went yesterday.
Pam	6 ?
Mary	50p.
Pam	Can I come with you?
Mary	Yes.
Pam	I'll just go and ask my dad. (A few minutes later)
Mary	7 ?
Pam	He said, "yes". But I've got to take my cousin, Percy.
Mary	8 ?
Pam	He's awful.
Mary	He can't be that bad.
Pam	Oh here he is.
Mary	Help! I'm off.

CLOZE

Questions:

1. What do you call a sleeping bull?
2. What can run but never walks?
3. What has six legs but only walks with four?
4. Why is a traffic policeman strong?
5. What is easy to get into but hard to get out of?
6. What is full of holes but holds water?
7. What has a neck but no head?
8. What kind of coat is always put on wet?
9. What starts with "T" ends with "T", and is full of "Tea"?
10. What has teeth but never eats?

What to do

Match the question with its answer.
Write your answer like this: *1. E*

Answers:

A. A teapot
B. Because he holds up the traffic
C. A coat of paint
D. A comb
E. A bulldozer
F. A tap
G. Trouble
H. A bottle
I. A sponge
J. A horse and rider

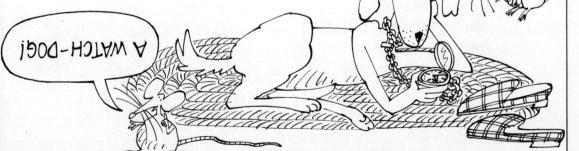

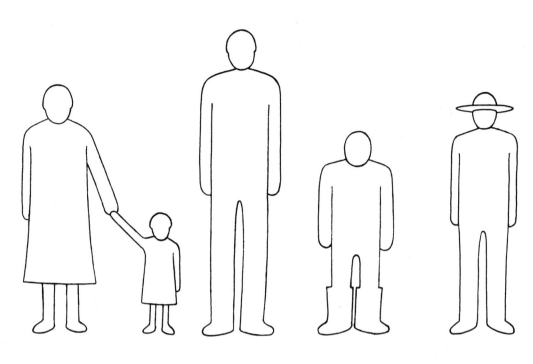

What to do

Copy this picture.   Colour it in.   Label the members of the family.   But read **all** of the page first.

The Globs

There are five people in the family: Mr and Mrs Glob and their three children, Tom, Jane and Mary.   Mrs Glob is taller than her husband.   Mary is smaller than her sister Jane.

Jane is wearing green jeans and a hat to match.   Her pullover is red.

Mr Glob is wearing a green pullover and red trousers.   He is wearing odd wellingtons.   His left one is red but his right one is green.

Tom is wearing black boots, a yellow pullover and blue trousers.

Mary's dress has yellow and black stripes like a wasp.   Her mother's dress is white with black dots.   Mrs Glob is wearing a blue wig.   Mr Glob is bald.   Both girls have black hair, but Tom's is red.

DEDUCTION

What to do

Find the missing words.

Anne has got a very ___1___ pet. He is a dinosaur. She ___2___ him in a raffle. Her pet is called Billy. Every day Anne takes Billy for a ___3___. Billy gets upset when he sees everybody run away when he comes into view. He does not know that ___4___ are afraid of dinosaurs.

Anne ___5___ Billy curry for his tea. He eats 1,427 bowls of curry ___6___ week. Billy likes rice too. He eats 150 kilos of rice a day.

Billy sleeps in ___7___ back yard. When he snores, all the ___8___ fall off the roof. His snoring keeps the neighbours awake. They have told Anne to ___9___ Billy.

The ___10___ have told Anne not to take Billy out on the street. Billy's huge feet make deep holes on the pavement. Billy has a ___11___ habit of sitting on cars. This squashes them flat like ___12___. Sometimes he sits on them when the drivers are inside!

People come from all over the ___13___ to see Billy. He tries to shake hands with everyone he meets. They run away as ___14___ as they can.

Anne is ___15___ Billy a scarf for his birthday. It is 124 metres long.

Logums

Logums come from the planet Dentol.   They are very large.   A logum has a body like an elephant.   Its neck is short and its head is quite small.   It has four short thick legs.   Its feet are flat.   Each foot has three big square toes.   A logum has a long trunk like an elephant.   The trunk turns up at the end.   There are two small nostrils in the end of the trunk. Under the trunk is a very long mouth.   Four sharp teeth stick down from the top jaw, like tusks.

The logum's eyes are small and round.   Its ears are small and pointed. They stand up on the top of the head and are close together.

The logum has long, thick green hair all over its body.   It lives in a cold climate.   This hair can be used to make clothes.

The logum is a slow-moving animal.   It is not easy to tame but it can be used to pull and carry heavy loads.

It has poor all round vision and poor hearing.

It is a meat eater.

> **What to do**
>
> Read the description of the logum.
> Draw a logum.
> Label the drawing.

Pindocks

> **What to do**
>
> This is a picture of a pindock.
> Write a description of a pindock
> like the description of the
> logum.

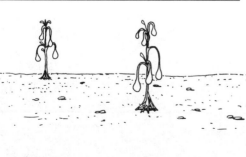

0   SCALE   1 metre

DRAWING

What to do

Here are some instructions that tell you how to make cheese on toast. Put them in the right order.

A. Cover the buttered side with grated cheese.
Put the bread and cheese back under the grill.

B. Get some cheese, butter and bread.
Thick, sliced bread is best. Put a slice of bread under the grill.

C. When the cheese melts, remove the toasted cheese from under the grill. Don't let the cheese burn. It should be golden brown.

D. Toast one side only. Take the bread from under the grill.
Grate some cheese.
Hard, tasty cheese is best for cheese on toast.

E. Butter the **untoasted** side of the slice of bread. Don't use too much butter or the bread will go soggy.

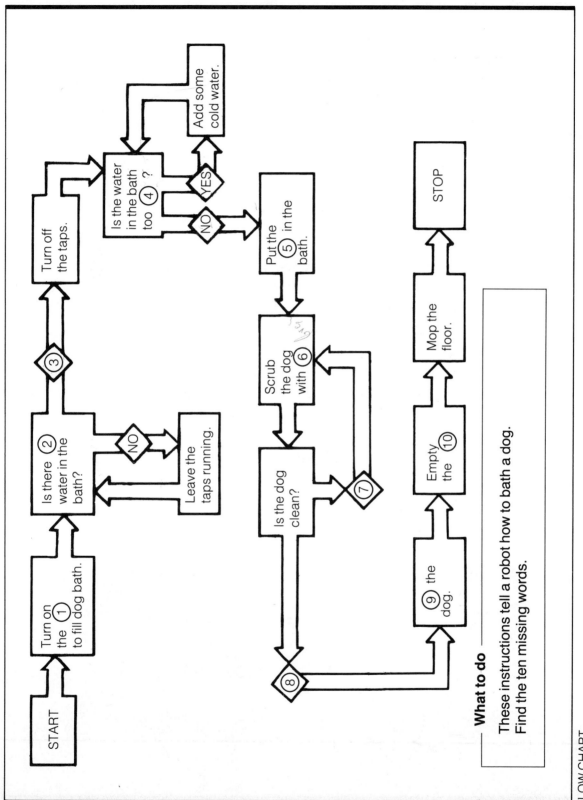

Add some cold water.

Turn off the taps.

Is the water in the bath too ④ ?

YES

NO

Put the ⑤ in the bath.

START

Turn on the ① to fill dog bath.

③

Is there water in the bath?

NO

Leave the taps running.

Scrub the dog with ⑥

Is the dog clean?

⑦

STOP

Mop the floor.

Empty the ⑩

⑨ the dog.

⑧

What to do

These instructions tell a robot how to bath a dog.
Find the ten missing words.

What to do

Who said what?   Match the words with the balloons.   Write your answers like this: 1. *C*

A. Ouch! My leg!

B. Can you see it?

C. Hello Deb.   Where's your bike?

D. And here's my stolen bike too.

E. Jump on.   I'll give you a lift.

F. Mind that dog Sally!

G. Here it is Deb.   I've found it.

H. No, the water is as black as ink.

I. Never mind your leg.   What about my bike?

J. Thanks.   Let's go down to the canal.

K. Oh no!

L. Somebody stole it last night.

MATCHING

What to do

Look at these pairs of pictures.
Think of **one word** to put in each of these sentences.

1. A + J   Both have got four _____ .
2. E + F   Both can _____ you if you are careless.
3. B + D   Both can _____ on water.
4. C + H   Both can be made from _____ .
5. A + I   Both might be made from _____ .
6. H + F   Both might be used by a _____ .
7. I + G   Both might be used by a _____ .
8. D + I   Both could help you to cross a _____ .
9. G + A   Both could help you to get over a _____ .
10. C + J   Both can get wet and _____ .

11. Which can you stand under?
12. Which can you stand on?
13. Which could you hide under?
14. Which could you send a message in?
15. Which could you hide in a match box?
16. Which **three things** could you put in a suit case?
17. Which **three things** all have parts you sit on?
18. Which **four things** all have parts made from metal?
19. Which would you give your granny for her birthday?
20. Which would you give your worst enemy for his/her birthday?

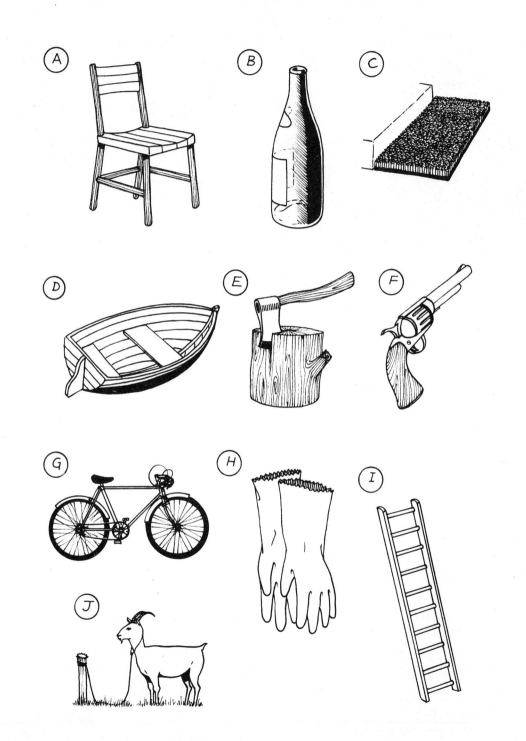

What to do

Find the missing words.

There was an old lion who was too old to hunt.　How could he get his
　　　1　　　?　He thought of a clever　　　2　　　.　He put a sign
on his door.　It said:
"I am　　　3　　　.　Please come and visit me before I die."

So all the animals went to see the old lion.　First to　　　4　　　was a
sheep.　Then a cow, then a rabbit, then a deer, then a donkey, and last of
all a young goat.　After each visitor, the　　　5　　　felt better.　He
　　　6　　　his lips, and smiled a sly smile.

Now the fox was the　　　7　　　animal who would not visit the lion.
This made the lion　　　8　　　.　At last the fox　　　9　　　go to
the lion's house.　But he would not go　　　10　　　.　The lion
begged him to come inside.

The fox said: "No thank you.　I don't want to come in."
"　　　11　　?" said the old lion.
The fox pointed to the footprints all around the lion's　　　12　　　.
Then he said to the lion:
"Look at these footprints.　They all lead　　　13　　　your cave, but
none of them lead　　　14　　　.　When all your visitors come
　　　15　　　, then I will come in to visit you!"

Moral:
Teeth are sharp but eyes are sharper.

What to do

Fill in the missing words.   Look at the picture very carefully.   Write the missing words only.

Ibbo cannot go in the house because his ___1___ tear up the carpets.   He has to stay in the ___2___ .   Ibbo doesn't like this because he gets ___3___ having no one to talk to.   Besides, it's very ___4___ in the garage and this makes Ibbo rusty.

Ibbo ___5___ all the letters but he cannot ___6___ the envelopes down because he has no tongue.

Ibbo can do ___7___ things at once.   He can work in the ___8___ because of the light on his head.

His owner is thinking of taking the garden fork and lawn mower from Ibbo's ___9___ .   He wants Ibbo to be able to work ___10___ the house.   Ibbo tried to mix a cake once, but he used his wrong arm and the cake mix ended up inside the ___11___ . Last week something went wrong with Ibbo's controls.   He went round drilling ___12___ in everything.   The furniture looked as if it had woodworm.

CLOZE

What to do

Here are some instructions that tell you how to clean a pair of shoes.   Put them in the right order.

A. An old brush is best for this.   Use the polish brush to give both shoes a thin coat of polish.   Do not use too much polish.

B. Put away the polish, brushes and rag.   Throw away the dirty newspaper.

C. Place the shoes on the newspaper.   If the shoes have laces, then take these out.   If the shoes are very muddy, clean the mud off.

D. Get the shoes, some polish, brushes and a rag.   Spread some old newspaper on the table before you start.

E. Let this polish dry.   Then polish the shoes with the rag.   Replace the laces.

SEQUENCING

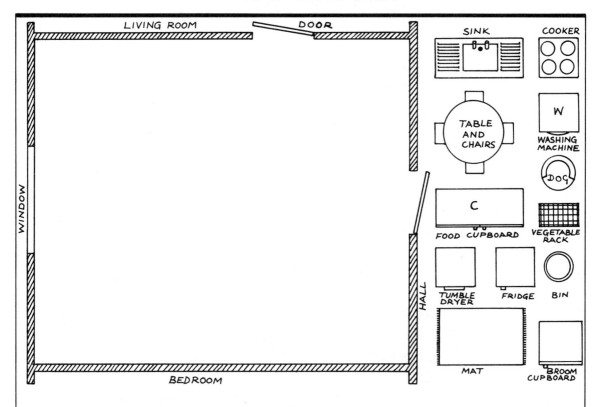

What to do

Draw or trace the plan of the kitchen.
Put all the things in their right place on your plan.

1. The dryer is against the wall opposite the living room door.
2. The sink is in front of the window.
3. The bin is on the left of the living room door.
4. The cooker is next to the bin, against the wall.
5. The washing machine is between the cooker and the sink.
6. The fridge is on the right of the dryer.
7. The broom cupboard is in the corner near the fridge.
8. The table and chairs are in the middle of the room.
9. The mat is in front of the sink.
10. The food cupboard is against the wall opposite the washing machine.
11. The vegetable rack is between the dryer and the food cupboard.
12. The dog basket is in the corner on the right of the living room door.

DRAWING

A. A long time ago, on the Island of Crete lived a white bull. This bull had silver horns. It was a beautiful animal, but it was very fierce and dangerous. The people who lived on the Island of Crete were afraid of the bull. It killed the animals on the island. Sometimes it killed people.

What to do

This is the first part of a story about Hercules. In this story Hercules is sent to Crete by the king. He catches a wild bull and brings it back alive.

Can you put the other six parts of the story in the right order?

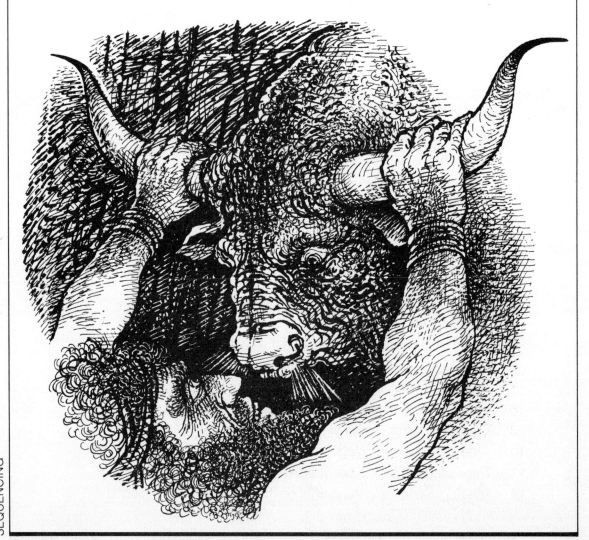

B. At last Hercules wanted to go back to Greece. He went down to the shore, but the ship had sailed away. "Now what shall I do?" thought Hercules. Then he had an idea. Hercules climbed on the bull's back, and the bull swam across the sea. Soon they reached Greece, and Hercules went back to the king with the bull. The king gave Hercules another task.

C. Hercules threw his club to the ground. The bull was very fierce, but Hercules was not afraid. He fought the bull, and at last he won. He pulled the bull to the ground by its horns. Hercules was stronger than the bull. He held it on the ground for a long time. The bull was afraid of Hercules. It was not fierce any more.

D. Hercules went into the forest. He hid in some bushes near a spring and waited. Soon he heard a loud noise. Then he saw something white through the trees. It was the fierce, white bull.

Just then the bull saw Hercules near the spring. It made a loud noise and attacked him.

E. Hercules climbed into a ship and sailed across the sea. After many days in the ship, Hercules saw an island. "It is the Island of Crete," thought he. "The white bull lives on that island."

Hercules jumped out of the ship, and walked on to the shore.

F. The king sent Hercules to Crete to capture the bull. The king said to Hercules, "You must not kill the bull. You must bring it back alive."

"This is a very hard task," thought Hercules as he picked up his club.

G. There was a forest on the island. In the forest there were a lot of tall trees. The sun shone through the trees, and it was very beautiful.

"The bull must be in this forest," thought Hercules.

SEQUENCING

What to do

Who said what?   Match the words with the balloons.
Write your answers like this: 1. *D*

A. Don't worry Sam, I'll get him down.
B. Oh no!   Not again!
C. Yes, get hold of the other end of the ladder.
D. Mum, Tiger's stuck up a tree.
E. Can I help?
F. Phone the fire brigade.
G. What are we going to do?
H. Be careful mum.   Oh dear!
I. What shall I do, mum?
J. Can you reach him, mum?
K. Look out Sam.   Stand back.
L. Not quite.   I'll have to climb along the branch.

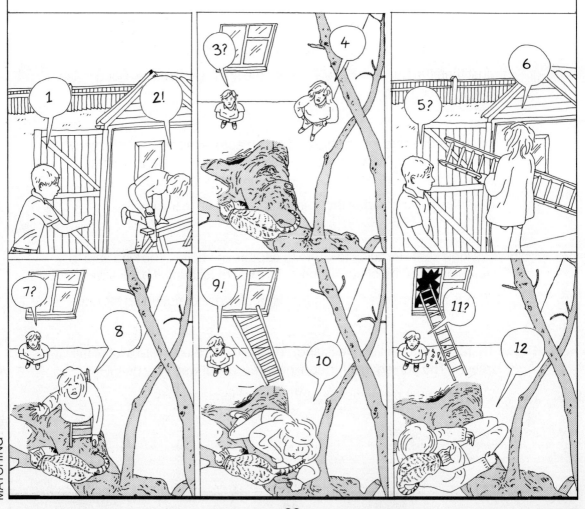

MATCHING

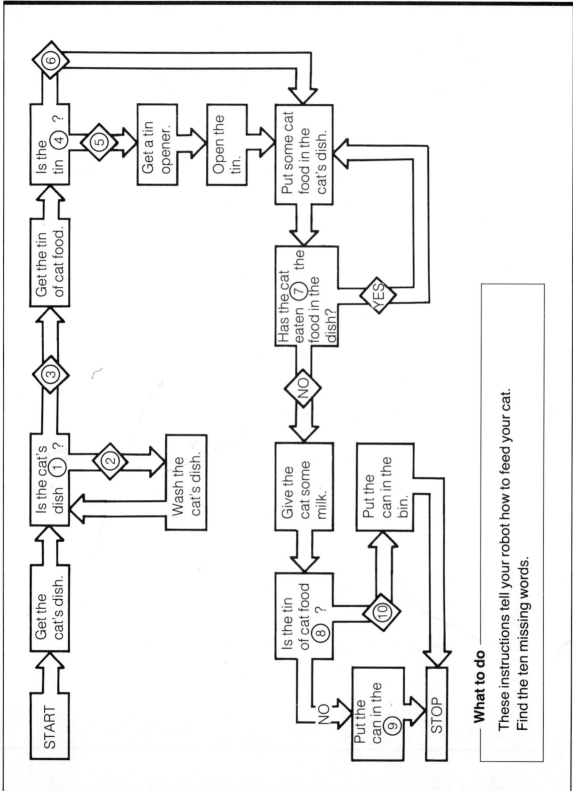

START

Get the cat's dish.

Is the cat's dish ① ?

② →

Wash the cat's dish.

③

Get the tin of cat food.

Is the tin ④ ?

⑤ →

Get a tin opener.

Open the tin.

⑥

Put some cat food in the cat's dish.

Has the cat eaten ⑦ the food in the dish?

YES

NO

Give the cat some milk.

Is the tin of cat food ⑧ ?

NO

Put the can in the ⑨

⑩

Put the can in the bin.

STOP

What to do

These instructions tell your robot how to feed your cat.

Find the ten missing words.

What to do

Answer true (T), false (F) or not enough evidence (NEE).

1. The railway station is in the centre of the town.
2. The battlefield is near a stream.
3. The main road through the town is very busy.
4. There is a chemist's shop near the church.
5. There is a footpath from the church to the canal.
6. There is a footpath from the lighthouse to the park.
7. The school has a large football field.
8. If you go from the town hall to the church you must cross the canal.
9. There is a swimming pool near the school.
10. The main road goes over the canal near the town hall.
11. Most of the houses in the town are old.
12. The canal goes over the railway just outside the town.
13. The cliffs are very dangerous.
14. There are three footpaths through the wood.
15. There is a picnic spot in the park.
16. The lighthouse is south of the town.
17. The stream from the lake flows north into the sea.
18. The church is west of the cemetery.
19. If you walked west along the coast from the cliffs you would come to a fun-fair.
20. The canal goes over the railway to the east of the town.

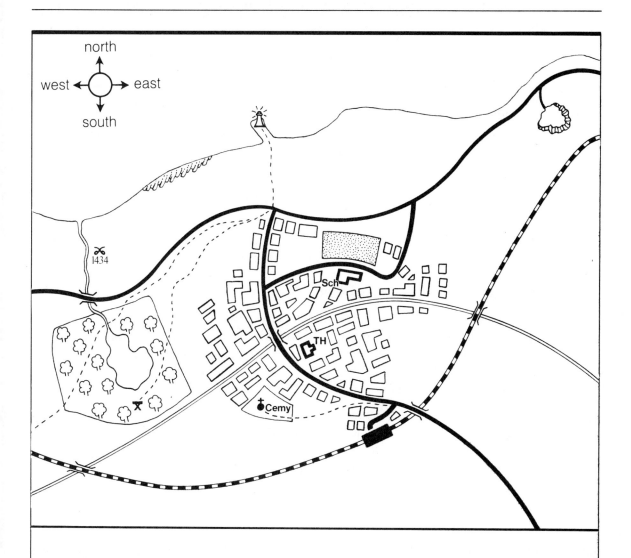

north
west ← → east
south

KEY.

🗿	. . . . quarry		▮▯▮	. . . . bridge	
〰	. . . . lake		〰〰	. . . . cliff	
✂	. . . . battlefield		Cemy	. . . . cemetery	
🗼	. . . . lighthouse		🌳 🌳	. . . . wood	
☘	. . . . church		▭	. . . . park	
- - -	. . . . footpath		⬛TH	. . . . Town Hall	
▬▬	. . . . road		⬛Sch	. . . . school	
▭▭	. . . . canal		✗	. . . . picnic spot	
▰▱▰	. . . . railway		▭	. . . . buildings	
▰◼▰	. . . . station				

DEDUCTION

What to do

Find the missing words.

Two ___1___ from Earth landed on a strange planet.   The strange ___2___ who lived there came out to meet them.   The spacewomen were a bit ___3___ .

But the creatures were very ___4___ .   They took the women to their ___5___ .   They gave them some food.   The women laughed when they saw the creatures eating.   They used two ___6___ and two forks at once!   They ate two different kinds of food at the same time.

The spacewomen had brought some gifts from Earth.   When they gave them to the creatures they laughed.   The explorers had brought some gloves and some pullovers.   The gloves were no use because the creatures only had ___7___ fingers on each hand.   The ___8___ were useless because all the creatures had four arms.

One of the creatures went back to ___9___ with the spacewomen.   The creature took part in the Olympic Games.   The crowd laughed when they saw the creature ___10___ a javelin, a shot, a hammer and discus all at the same time!   The creature won four gold medals.

CLOZE

42

Fengol

Fengol is a planet deep in outer space.
It is a strange place.   It is very different from Earth.   It is always very dark on Fengol because black clouds hide the sun.   It is never sunny but it is very warm because the rocks on Fengol are very hot.   You can fry an egg on them.
Fengol has many rivers.   These rivers are very wide and very slow.   The river water is pure but it is very hot – too hot for fish or plants.
Fengol has many thick forests.   The trees are all very tall.   They have red leaves.
Most of the strange animals on Fengol live in the tree tops.   Some animals are very dangerous.
The atmosphere on Fengol is poisonous for humans.

What to do

You have to go to Fengol to make a film of the animals there.
What would you take with you?
Pick six things from the list that you *must* take.
Pick six things that would *not* be useful on Fengol.

   Give a reason for each choice.

1. A motor bike
2. A fishing rod
3. A fridge
4. A folding table
5. Camera and film

6. A folding boat
7. Cigarettes
8. Some food
9. Thick boots
10. Thick pullovers

11. Batteries
12. Air tanks
13. Folding ladders
14. Postage stamps
15. Sun glasses

16. A red overall
17. A gun
18. Powerful lamps
19. A football
20. A jeep

DEDUCTION

Answer true (T), false (F) or not enough evidence (NEE).

1. Two girls rescued the baby.
2. A fireman had to climb onto the ledge to help the girls.
3. The baby climbed out of a window in a first floor flat.
4. It was a very windy day.
5. The baby was a girl.
6. The baby was smiling when she was rescued.
7. The old lady got hold of the baby's leg.
8. The firemen held out a safety net.
9. Both the girls had long hair.
10. The fireman's ladder was not long enough to reach the ledge.
11. The girl had the walking stick in her right hand.
12. The flats are eight storeys high.
13. Both the girls were wearing jeans.
14. The old woman holding onto the old man is the baby's granny.
15. The woman is holding out her umbrella to keep the baby dry.
16. The firemen could not put their ladders up because it was too windy.
17. The two girls got up onto the roof by using the fireman's ladders.
18. The baby dropped the teddy bear.
19. The girl hooked the walking stick round the baby's arm.
20. The woman with the umbrella is the caretaker's wife.

What to do next

BRAVE BEAR BABY FIREMEN WHILE
RESCUE TEDDY GIRLS RESCUE

These 9 words can be arranged to make a headline for a newspaper story.   Put them in the right order.   Then write a short report to go with the headline.

DEDUCTION

What to do

What are these people talking about?
Each pair is talking about the *same* thing.

1. **Doctor**   They can make you ill. They may even kill you.
    Tobacconist   I sell hundreds of these every week.

2. **Customs officer**   I have to check hundreds of these every day.
    Travellers   We have to take these with us if we leave the country.

3. **Farmer**   It will kill my crops.
    Skier   It's just what I've been waiting for.

4. **Gambler**   I can win or lose money with these.
    Magician   I can use these to do tricks.

5. **Music students**   We need them to practise on.
    Removal man   I hate moving these – they are so heavy.

6. **Gardener**   They help me in the garden.
    Fisherman   I use them for bait.

7. **Thief**   I must not leave these behind.
    Detective   I must look for these at the scene of the crime.

8. **Nurse**   I use this to save lives.
    Dracula   I have it for breakfast!

9. **Boy or girl**   This keeps my bike safe.
    Thief   This keeps me out.

10. **Elderly person**   They are noisy and dangerous.
    Young person   They are great fun.

11. **Lollipop woman**   It's where I go every day to work.
    A small boy or girl   It can be a dangerous place for me.

12. **Grave digger**   This is where I work.
    Film director   This is a good place to make a horror film.

Mary

Mary worked in a fish shop.
She did not like it much.   She wanted a job in an office, like the
rest of her mates.   But she could not **type**.   One day at the
shop she was cleaning a big silver fish.   Some fish **scales** went
in her **right** eye.   She had to go to the doctor.   The doctor said:
>   "Oh dear . . . the **tip** of a scale has got into your **pupil**.   Hold
>   still while I get it out."

The next day Mary's eye was as red as a **rose** and very sore.
Now, to be on the **safe** side, she always wears her glasses when
she is cleaning fish.

Tom

Tom was a biology teacher.
One day he brought a snake into school.   It had rose red scales
and green eyes.
Tom asked a first year pupil if she would look after it for him.
The pupil said:
>   "Is it safe, sir?"

Tom laughed and said:
>   "Oh yes!   This type of snake is quite harmless.   I'll show
>   you the right way to pick it up."

Then Tom got hold of the snake by the tip of its tail.   The snake
bit Tom on his arm.   He was off school for the rest of the term.

What to do

The 8 words in the table are
in both stories.
Copy the table.
Show if these 8 words have
the **same** or **different**
meanings by putting ticks in
the table.

	same	different
rest		
type		
scales		
right		
tip		
pupil		
rose		
safe		

HOMONYMS

A lion was sleeping in his den.   A mouse ran into the den.   It ran up onto the lion's head and sat on its nose.   The lion woke up.   It was very angry.   It grabbed the mouse in its mighty paw.

"How dare you wake me up!   I'll kill you for this!" roared the lion. The mouse was very scared.   It said:

"Please don't eat me.   Please let me go.   I did not mean to wake you up.   If you let me go, who knows, maybe one day I will be able to help you."

When the lion heard this, it laughed.   It thought it was a great joke.   How could a skinny little mouse help the King of Beasts?   But he let the little mouse go free, and the mouse ran as fast as it could out of the den.

A few days later, the mouse was out looking for food.   It came upon the lion caught up in a big net.   The net was a trap, set by hunters.   The lion struggled to get free.   But the more it struggled, the tighter the net became.

"Lie still," said the mouse to the lion.

Then the mouse bit a small hole in the net with its sharp teeth.   The mouse chewed and chewed and chewed.   Soon the small hole was big enough for the lion to put its paw through.   Soon the lion had two paws free.   The mouse kept chewing and chewing at the net, and soon the lion was free from the trap.

"There," said the mouse, "that's how a little mouse can help a great lion."

What to do

Here are five summaries of the story.   Only one summary is the same as the story.   Find the summary that fits the story best.   Say what is wrong with the other four summaries.

1.   The story is about a mouse who proved he was as strong as a stupid lion.

2.   The story is about a cunning lion who promised to help a mouse but did not.

3.   The story is about a clever mouse who helped some hunters trap a lion.

4.   This story is about a clever mouse who helps a lion to get out of a trap.

5.   This is a story about a clever mouse who gets his own back on a cruel lion.

1.   Mr Peters was dead.

2.   The car in the garage had been stolen.

3.   Someone had broken into the garage.

4.   The robber got away through the park.

5.   Mr Peters was asleep when he saw the robber.

6.   The robber was trying to steal the car.

7.   Mr Peters told the police what the attacker was wearing.

8.   Mr Peters was mending his car when he was attacked.

9.   The robber was wearing a red woollen pullover.

10.   The robber cut his hand when he broke into the garage.

11.   The robber could not get Mr Peters' car to start.

12.   The robber dropped his gloves next to the bunch of keys.

13.   Mr Peters was much stronger than the robber.

14.   Mr Peters jumped on the robber before the robber opened the garage.

15.   The robber got into the garage but he could not get into the car.

DEDUCTION

story A

There was once a farmer who had a big farm near a wood. A fox lived in the wood. Every night this fox would creep out of its den and steal one of the farmer's hens. This went on for two years. The farmer tried many times to catch the fox but could not. The fox was clever.

One day, however, the fox got careless. The farmer caught it and put it in a box. The farmer wanted to kill the fox but in a cruel way. He tied a bundle of thin sticks to the fox's tail and set fire to it. Then he set the fox free. The fox ran right through the farmer's field of ripe corn. The corn was set on fire and burnt up. The fox jumped into the river and ran off, free as a bird.

story B

A farmer had a small farm near a stream. He had lots of hens on his farm and cows and pigs. There was a fox who lived near by. Every night it came to the farm and stole a hen. The farmer tried to shoot the fox but he was a poor shot and his gun was old.

One day, the fox got stuck in some barbed wire. The farmer saw it and put it in a sack. The farmer's son was kind. He wanted to save the fox. But the farmer tried to kill it. He tied some straw to the fox's tail and set it on fire. The fox escaped and ran into the farmer's corn field. The field caught fire, and so did the farmer's barn. The fox escaped with a burnt tail.

What to do

The two stories are nearly the same but not quite! In which story did you read this?

Copy this part of the table and finish it off.

		story A	story B
1. The farmer had a big farm.	1	✓	✗
2. The fox lived near the farm.	2		
3. The farmer kept hens.	3		
4. The farmer kept pigs.	4		
5. The farmer put the fox in a box.	5		
6. The farmer tied the fox to a tree.	6		
7. The farmer's son tried to save the fox.	7		
8. The farmer tied some twigs to the fox's tail.	8		
9. The farmer shot the fox.	9		
10. The fox jumped into the river.	10		

COMPARISONS

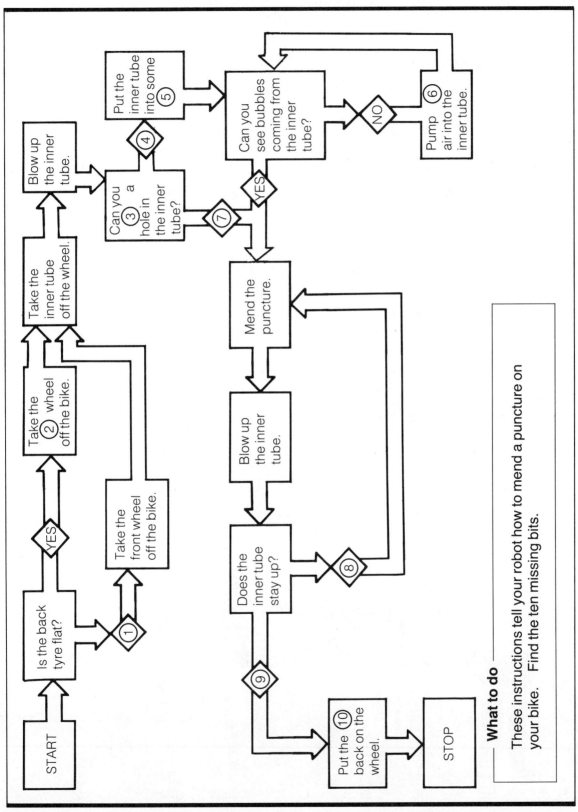

START

Is the back tyre flat?

① YES

Take the ② wheel off the bike.

Take the front wheel off the bike.

Take the inner tube off the wheel.

Blow up the inner tube.

④ Put the inner tube into some

③ Can you a hole in the inner tube?

⑦

Can you see bubbles coming from the inner tube?

NO

⑥ Pump air into the inner tube.

YES

Mend the puncture.

Blow up the inner tube.

Does the inner tube stay up?

⑧

⑨

Put the ⑩ back on the wheel.

STOP

What to do

These instructions tell your robot how to mend a puncture on your bike. Find the ten missing bits.

FLOW CHART

What to do

Here are some instructions that tell you how to use a pay 'phone (a public telephone).
Put them in the right order.

A. Pick up the receiver.   Listen for the dialling tone – this is a purring sound.   If there is no dialling tone, then the 'phone is out of order.

B. When you hear the dialling tone, dial your friend's number. After a second or two, you will hear your friend's 'phone ringing.

C. Make sure you have the right change.   If you are not sure of the number, look in the directory or ask the operator to help you.

D. If your friend does not answer, or their 'phone is engaged, then replace the receiver.   Try again in a few minutes.

E. When your friend answers, you will hear the pay pips.   Press your money into the pay slot.   Then speak.

Aunt Georgina

Aunt Georgina came round one **fine** July day. She needed a **set** of tools. I said she could borrow **mine**. She said she was making something interesting. I had some **free** time because it was my holidays, so I asked her if I could help. She took me to her garage. She was making a car. I was very surprised. She said:
   "You can do anything if you put your **mind** to it!"
Two days later, all the car needed was a front **light** and someone to mend a **flat** tyre. We went for a drive up the motorway. Aunt Georgina drove so fast that I had to **hold** on tight. But we got stuck in a traffic **jam**. There was a loud bang. The engine stopped. Aunt Georgina looked under the bonnet. She knew just what to do.
   "It's the **fan** belt," she said. "I'll mend it with my tights."

Uncle Bill

Uncle Bill was a miner. One day he was working down the mine, fixing an electric fan. Suddenly his mate, Kenny, shouted:
   "Mind out, Bill! Rock fall!"
But the warning came too late. Bill was trapped. The light was very dim. The air was full of fine, black dust. Bill was choking. Kenny pulled him free, then went for help. Uncle Bill was taken to hospital. The doctor gave him an injection. This made him dream. In his dream, men with white coats grabbed hold of him and put strawberry jam all over his arm. The jam set hard, like cement. Then Bill woke up. He was flat on his back in a hospital bed with his arm in plaster!

	same	different
fine		
set		
mine		
free		
mind		
light		
flat		
hold		
jam		
fan		

What to do

The 10 words in the table are in both stories.
Copy the table.
Show if these 10 words have the **same** or **different** meanings by putting ticks in the table.

HOMONYMS

A rich man lost his wallet.
He said he would give a reward to anyone who found it.   There was £100 in the wallet.   The rich man said:

"If anyone finds the wallet and brings it to me I will give them £50."

A poor man found the wallet.   He took it to the rich man to get the reward.   The rich man did not want to give the poor man the £50 so he said:

"When I lost my wallet there was a large ruby in it.   Give me back my ruby . . . then you will get your reward!"

The poor man knew the rich man was not telling the truth.   The two men went to a judge, to see if she could settle the argument.
When the judge heard what the poor man had to say, she said to the rich man:

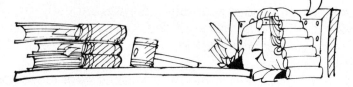

"You say there was a large ruby and £100 in your wallet. Well, there is no ruby in this wallet so it cannot be yours.   This poor man can keep this wallet until its owner is found."

When he heard this, the rich man stopped arguing and gave the poor man his £50.

What to do

Here are five summaries of the story.   Which summary best describes what happened in the story?   Say what is wrong with the other four summaries.

---

1. This story is about a poor man who steals a rich man's wallet.
2. This story is about a rich man and a poor man who argue over a wallet.
3. This story is about a poor man who tries to cheat a rich man.
4. This is a story about how a judge stops a rich man from cheating a poor man.
5. This is the story of a rich man who loses a ruby.   A poor man finds it, but will not give it back.

Ifs:

A. everyone went deaf?

B. everyone went bald?

C. steel became soft?

D. water became sticky?

E. nothing would burn?

Consequences:

1. swimming baths would close down

2. more lip reading

3. ducks could not take off from ponds

4. no need for firemen

5. no telephones

6. wig makers would get rich

7. knives would be blunt

8. barbers would be poor

9. boats would go slower

10. no radio

11. no combs

12. more trees

13. no music

14. no gas stoves

15. pylons would fall down

16. everyone's head would look the same from behind

17. snow would be sticky

18. trains would crash

19. some zips would not work

20. no more fireworks

What to do

Match the 'ifs' with their consequences.

Write your answers like this: A. 2   A. 5   A .....

RIDDLES

Once, in a far off country, there lived a powerful queen.   One day, she fell ill.   She was very sick, but nobody knew why.   The wisest men and women came to see the queen.   They all tried to cure her, but they failed.

Then one day, a young girl came to the queen's house.
She said she knew how to cure the queen's sickness.
She said:
> "If the queen can find a happy man and take his shirt and put it on, then she will be cured."

So the queen sent all her servants to search for a happy man.   But they could not find anyone who was completely happy.

Now the queen was on her death bed.   She might die any day.
Her daughter was very sad.   She said:
> "There must be *one* happy man in the country.   I will go and search for him myself."

Later that night, the queen's daughter was passing by a tiny cottage.   She heard a man say to his son:
> "Well my son, I have finished my work, I have eaten my fill, and now I can lie down and have a good night's sleep.
> What more could I want?"

The queen's daughter went up to the man and said:
> "Please will you give me your shirt?   I must take it to the queen."

But the happy man was so poor that he did not own a shirt, and the queen's daughter had to go away empty handed.

What to do

Which summary best describes what happened in the story?   Say what is wrong with the other five summaries.

---

1. This is a story about a poor man who tries to help the queen's daughter.

2. This is a story about a powerful queen who goes in search of a poor man's shirt.

3. This is a story about a shirt with magic powers that can make poor people happy.

4. The story is about the daughter of a queen who is tricked by a poor man.

5. This is a story about a daughter who tries to find the cure for her mother's strange illness.

6. This is the story of how a young girl tries to make a sick queen happy.

SUMMARY

story A

A donkey was resting in a field when she saw a wolf creeping along behind the hedge.   The donkey had never seen the wolf before but she knew the wolf wanted to attack her and eat her. The donkey was clever.   When the wolf came near, the donkey started to limp.

"I have stood on a thorn," said the donkey to the wolf.   "If you eat me, the thorn will stick in your throat and kill you.   Please pull it out with your long, sharp teeth."
The wolf smiled a sly smile.   He thought the donkey was so stupid!

He put his mouth to the donkey's foot.   But the donkey kicked out with all her might.   All the wolf's teeth were broken.   The donkey trotted off, laughing and laughing.

story B

A donkey was resting by a stream when she heard a wolf creeping along under the hedge nearby.   The wolf was the donkey's enemy.   For years, the wolf had been trying to trap the donkey and eat her.   But the donkey was clever.

After a while, the wolf slipped out of the hedge and came towards the donkey.   Just then, the donkey started to cry She rolled over and over saying,

"Oh my foot, oh my foot.   There's a sharp nail in my foot.   Please Mr Wolf can you pull it out for me?   If you don't and you eat me, you will choke on it."

The wolf was only too happy to help the donkey.   He put his long, sharp claws on the donkey's foot.   The donkey kicked out and knocked the wolf unconscious.   The donkey ran off, laughing and laughing.

What to do

The two stories are nearly the same – but not quite!
In which story did you read this?

Copy this and finish it off

		story A	story B
1. The wolf crept up on the donkey.	1	✓	✓
2. The donkey was near a lake.	2		
3. The wolf hid under the hedge.	3		
4. The donkey pretended she had a nail in her foot.	4		
5. The donkey pretended she had a thorn in her foot.	5		
6. The donkey asked the wolf for help.	6		
7. The wolf knew the donkey was playing a trick on him.	7		
8. The wolf put his mouth near the donkey's foot.	8		
9. The wolf was knocked out.	9		
10. The wolf ran after the donkey.	10		

COMPARISONS

This is what 15 pupils said about their school.
Copy the table and classify what the pupils said.

Copy this part.

		good things about our school	bad things about our school	things about lessons	things about friends
1.	I think this school is much too big.	1		✓		
2.	I don't like wearing school uniform.	2				
3.	I think our school dinners are smashing.	3				
4.	I wish we had a safe place to leave our bikes at school.	4				
5.	I like the school tuck-shop best.	5				
6.	I wish the teachers were a bit more friendly.	6				
7.	I have lots of mates at this school.	7				
8.	I don't like the teachers here much.	8				
9.	I think our form room is very dull and drab.	9				
10.	I wish we had smaller classes.	10				
11.	I didn't like my last school but I love it here.	11				
12.	I wish we had a swimming pool at our school.	12				
13.	I think the teachers try hard to help us.	13				
14.	I think the school is too old fashioned.	14				
15.	I like games but the rest of the lessons are boring.	15				

CLASSIFICATION

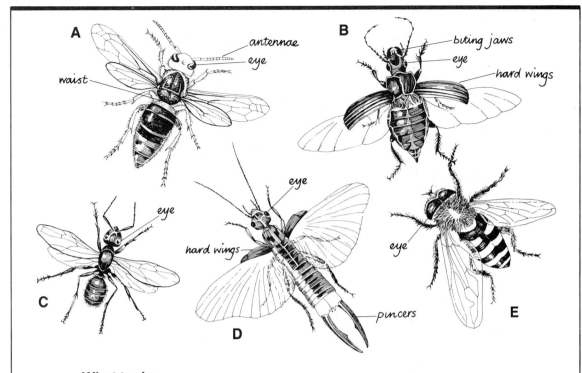

A — antennae, eye, waist
B — biting jaws, eye, hard wings
C — eye
D — eye, hard wings, pincers
E — eye

What to do

Copy this table and fill it in.

		A	B	C	D	E
		\multicolumn{5}{Copy this part.}				
1.	Only two wings	1	✗	✗	✗	✗	✓
2.	Six legs	2					
3.	Pincers	3					
4.	A long, thin body	4					
5.	Wings with veins	5					
6.	Long antennae and small eyes	6					
7.	Bent antennae and two hard wings	7					
8.	Big eyes and very small antennae	8					
9.	Four wings and a very thin waist	9					
10.	Four wings with the front wings bigger than the back ones	10					

CLASSIFICATION

What to do

Trace the Super-bike.   Read the description.   Then label the bike.

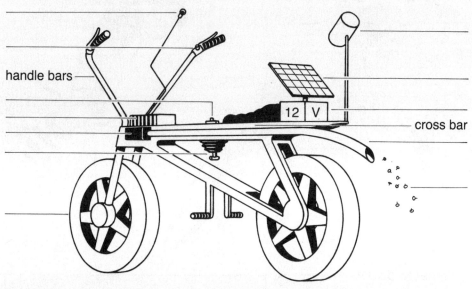

handle bars

12 V

cross bar

Why pedal when you can ride Sam's Super-bike?

The Super-bike is made for very lazy people.   The Super-bike is solar-powered.   There are no pedals!   There is a square solar panel above the bike seat.   This takes in energy from the sun.   It turns the back wheel.   The bike can still be used when it is cloudy.   Turn on the lamp with the switch on the cross bar.   The light shines onto the solar panel.   The light uses a 12 volt battery.   This is behind the seat.

There is a C.B. radio on the bike.   The radio is in a stripy box on the cross bar.   The microphone sticks out from the handle bars.

The wheels are made from strong plastic.   There is a pump hanging down from the cross bar.

Have you any enemies following you?   The Super-bike can get rid of them for you.   Just press the button on the handle bars.   Tacks will go down the cross bar and out of the tube at the back.   The tacks are stored in the black box on the cross bar.

What to do next

Is this a good idea for a bike?   Give a reason for your answer.
Design a Super-bike of your own.